Tiny Anchors

poems by

Sarah Hulsman

Finishing Line Press
Georgetown, Kentucky

Tiny Anchors

Copyright © 2021 by Sarah Hulsman
ISBN 978-1-64662-545-1 First Edition
All rights reserved under International and Pan-American Copyright Conventions. No part of this book may be reproduced in any manner whatsoever without written permission from the publisher, except in the case of brief quotations embodied in critical articles and reviews.

Publisher: Leah Huete de Maines

Editor: Christen Kincaid

Cover Art and Design: Amy Hulsman

Author Photo: Amy Hulsman

Order online: www.finishinglinepress.com
also available on amazon.com

Author inquiries and mail orders:
Finishing Line Press
PO Box 1626
Georgetown, Kentucky 40324
USA

Table of Contents

1 Conversations with Sheep

2 Please Get Home Safe

3 Tiny Anchors Part I

4 Reading

5 Plans

7 Co-Star

8 Tiny Anchors Part II

9 Mom

10 Icebreakers

12 Love Language

13 OCD

15 Dad

16 What's It Like?

18 Love Letter #1

23 Amy

24 Away Part I

25 Routine

26 Beautiful Wonderful

28 Diet Plan

29 Away Part II

31 Rest Stop

for the late bloomers

Conversations with Sheep

Today the scientists
disproved the theory
that counting sheep
helps us fall asleep.

They wrote up a study that claims
moonlighting as shepherds
activates a part of our brains
associated with processing information

and we would sleep much better
if we instead imagined
beautiful, made up scenes
like a beach or a mountain or

a sunny summer day
where everything we thought
was lost to us
came back home.

I've been doing my own research though.
Outlining my own findings.
It turns out that sheep
are great conversationalists.

We graze in a grassland made up of
all the places I should have gone but didn't
and all the plans I made but didn't follow.

We talk long into the night
about where the going wrong started
and how long the feeling bad might last.

Please Get Home Safe

You sent me
a goodnight text
at 1:00am last night
on your way home from
a party with your friends

and of all the rules
we're doomed to break
in this breakup
I'm sure that this one
is the sweetest.

Tiny Anchors Part I

Do you remember the night
we closed all the windows
and turned the sandman away?
Bargained with him
to skip your room
and leave us be?

Instead of magic sleep dust
you sprinkled question after question onto my body
and I whispered answers back into yours.

"Green"
"Taurus"
"November"
"A writer"
"My mom"

Now I think
you wanted to borrow little parts of me
and cast each one as a tiny anchor
to ground yourself against the wind
that was starting to take you away.

I know you tried to stay.

Reading

I'm probably reading too much
into your silence
but let
me
explain.

I was the kid
who spent most of her time
buried in book pages
searching for stories

and the remaining hours of the day
filling up notebooks
and summer air
and other people's time
with my own.

What else is there to do
with the quiet
except play make believe?

Plans

You said you're too busy for a relationship
so I'm working on a few plans.

The first is gathering up all the wasted time in the world
from each and every person
and gifting you your own 8th day per week
which is reserved for only
breakfast and reading and me.

The second is building a time machine
that takes me back to each moment you felt overwhelmed
so that right before the anxiety ignites in your body
I can blanket you with the reassurance
that I can be as light as a feather in your life.

The third and fourth go hand in hand.
You write me one list of everyone you've ever loved
and another of everyone you think could ever hurt you.
I'll gather both groups in one room
and we'll write a new constitution.

The fifth is waiting for you
and the sixth is moving on
neither of which sound appealing
or plausible or kind to either of us.
So I'll skip

ahead

to the 7th plan.
The grandest of them all.

I write a poem about you
and another
and then another.

I slowly pull your presence out of my body
and pin each line of it to a new piece of paper
which I then press into a book
and gently leave in the sunny section of a public library
where they house other stories
of lessons learned the hard way.

When you can depend on someone,
you won't feel the need to possess them.

Co-Star

Tonight Co-Star told me
"where there is emptiness, there is grace"
which is honestly the smartest thing she's told me since early June
back when I was so so so nervous to meet you
and I opened her before our first date
and she simply said
"jump."

Tiny Anchors Part II

and I know
you don't have a lot of time these days
to think about my replies
or to reconsider them
or want new ones.

But just in case the sandman
skips your room again tonight,
here's my last three:

Of course we can meet again in 6 months
if you can promise me you'll still want to.

I had a sad day
because I saw your profile on Hinge
even though we broke up
so you could prioritize loving yourself
and I spent the afternoon
jealous of all the new people
who get to meet you for the first time.

I could never hate you.
I rarely take the easy route.

Mom

Here is a poem
for my mama

who has held more of my spilled tears
than all of these pages combined

and who has listened to me talk myself
in and out of every heartbreak
this body has ever withstood.

I love you
and I know that I will be okay
and that I am strong
and that I can weather this sadness

because I have watched you weather your own

and there does not exist a world
where you quit

so neither will I.

Icebreakers

Most of the people in my life
have been introduced to my anxiety
in one way or another
but for you new folks,
I'll do a few icebreakers.

She was born
around the same time
that I attended my first funeral.
unplanned, of course,
but that's just what happens
when religion demands
10 years olds to cure cancer
using only the power of prayer.

She was raised lovingly by
Lack of Control and Heteronormativity.

She likes to eat daylight for breakfast.

Her dream car
is one that hits pedestrians
every time I turn right on a red.

Her favorite food
is when my ex watches my Instagram story
but doesn't text me back.

Her favorite movie
is any film from my childhood
where I can't exactly figure out
why the pretty leading lady
makes me so nervous.

Her favorite time of year
is August
not only because it's her birthday month
but also because it is the start of two of her favorite seasons:
death and wildfires.

Love Language

My love language
is staying out of the way.
is not making a sound.
is taking care of myself
so that you don't have to.

OCD

To the next person who declares
that they write neatly
because they're "so OCD"

Write me 500 words on
intrusive thoughts
and compulsions
and repetitions
and darkness
and worry.

See how those lines
cascade down the page
in a neat and orderly fashion?

Would you have assumed that
your mother was going to die
if you wrote them any different?

To the next person
who co-opts
a disease
in the name of
wanting to play quirky for a day

Walk a mile in my sister's shoes first,
but be careful not to step on any cracks
or lines
or leaves
or twigs

because you'll be spending the rest of the afternoon
stuck in a mind maze
remedying the catastrophic events
a stroll down the street can inflict.

To the next person
who grows annoyed at the constant throat clearing
or finger snapping
or light switching
or quiet murmuring

especially if that person is me

remember to practice your own repetition
empathy
compassion
grace
repeat.

Dad

My dad is a gardener.
A landscaper, by trade.
He wears fuschia
more than any other color.
He loves musicals and ABBA
and always plays as Princess Peach.

That's how I know
good men grow flowers from their chests.

My dad doesn't drink
and he never yells.
He spends most of his time outside
or watching politics in the den.
I've never seen him want for anything else
or ask the universe to bring new things to the door.

That's how I know
contentment is both a failing and a triumph.

My dad says "I love you" more
than he ever did when I was a kid.
I've watched him turn from a man who said
"If they can get married, then what's next?"
into a father who held his gay daughter on a couch
and promised to love her still, and love her more.

That's how I know
it's never too late to start anew.

What's It Like?

When you're doing The Work of
outlining what you currently know about yourself
unwinding why you didn't know it before
dancing around how to tell other people about your knowing

and traveling daily in a

one step
forward

two steps
backward

dance
between

repression and acceptance
bargaining and cultivation
shame and pride

you can lose sight of the happiness
that you're actively channeling
into your life

this new life

frankensteined from
the best of the old
and the promises of the new

What's it like
to finally come home to yourself?

It's finding a rest stop
when you've been driving on empty
for too long.

It's opening your book back up
to the exact right page
after you thought you lost your place.

It's successfully setting down
three armfuls of groceries
that you insisted you could carry in one fell swoop.

It's finally writing love letters
to all the versions of yourself
who have waited by the mailbox for so long.

Love Letter #1

Hessica will be the first one you tell.
It'll come out as more of a quiet suggestion
rather than a bold confession.
"I kissed a girl at a party last month."

You didn't
and you haven't, yet
but you will tell this lie to test the waters;
to see how safe an actual swim would be.

Her response of "Oh, yeah. I'd kiss a girl too"
will be the saving grace of your year
and her subsequent unwavering defense of your heart
will plant the first seedling of the idea

that this might not have to be A Bad Thing
because she will still love you.

Daniel will be the second one you tell,
years later.
You'll have let the truth inside now
slowly and carefully and methodically

and not nearly enough to even consider the
remote possibility of any outsider knowing.
But he is not an outsider.
He is one of your best friends.

You've held each other
as the worst of the world
came to your door, sniffing for blood.
And Daniel is gay, too.

Just like you.

So you begin a journey
of Daniel knowing.
Pretty soon, he will start talking about "our" community
and there will be rainbows hanging in your house

and he will stop asking you about boys
and start harassing you about any woman within a 50 mile radius
and slowly, this secret that you have spent years
repressing and ignoring and invalidating

has room to bloom into A Good Thing
nurtured by the fact that he will still love you.

The first girl you kiss
will be named Cecily.
You'll kiss her in your car
after bringing her out for drinks

at a bar in North Hollywood.
You normally will not be so bold
to suggest making out on the first date
but Trump will have just been elected two days prior

and kissing her
will feel like just about
the only thing you can do right now
to fight the hatred in the world.

That same Saturday night you'll go back home
with every emotion you've ever stifled
starting to swirl around inside of your body.
You'll watch Kate McKinnon sing Hallelujah

and you will wonder if your goosebumps
are from her nationally broadcast protest
or from the smaller one that you quietly led
in the backseat of your car earlier that evening.

It'll be a little over a year from then
until you decide to tell your next person.
Although "decide" is up for debate.
You'll be driving up home

along the 5
for the holiday with your family.
You'll start crying once you get to the 580
because the highway will be screaming that it's time.

Your family will never give you
a reason to think that you'll have your own version
of the horror stories you've heard
but telling them makes it Real.

and if Mom knows
you cannot hide the secret
within the borders of Los Angeles
if this whole thing ends up being a mistake.

First you'll tell your sister
because she's your best friend
and because there's nothing in the world that she could tell you
that you would not accept and defend as your own.

Next you'll sit Mom down on the couch
and you'll tell her
that the car accident you got into last month
happened on the way to meet a girl at a bar for a date

and she will sigh
which you'll think is disappointment
but it's relief
because she's known you were gay

since you were five
and she has loved you
more and more
each day of your existence.

So then you'll tell Dad
and after he scolds you
for making him jump to the conclusion
that your body is sick with any number of possible diseases

He will give you a big hug
the kind from your childhood
where he holds you to his chest
and he'll whisper you secrets of his own

and he will only stop when Mom yells from the kitchen
"The same dating rules apply, I will hit a woman!"
and you will laugh.
Really laugh.

because they will finally know
and they will never not know again
and November will become your favorite month
because they will still love you.

You'll tell Emma at a sushi place.
and she will still love you.
Gabby at a comedy show.
and she will still love you.

Ally on a walk through the neighborhood.
Anne Marie over the phone.
Cyrus in the middle of a three hour conversation.
Melissa outside of a Peruvian restaurant in San Francisco.

and despite everything you've worried about
all of the horrible possibilities that you've sketched out
they will not only love you despite.
they will love you more because.

and here
in all these tiny moments
is where the feeling bad starts to end.

Amy

Is there anything as healing
as laying on a bed

next to the person
you feel closest to in the world

knowing that
you are free to be

completely undone
not only because they will help piece you together

when the construction starts in the spring
but also because they will wait

and wait and wait and wait and wait and wait
until you are ready

to lay the first brick yourself.

Away Part I

What do you do
when you realize
you were the placeholder?
the stand in?
the distraction?
the "good for now"?
the wildflower that accidentally blooms in winter
while the gardener is waiting for her annuals
to pop back up?

You get to work.

You sleep them away
in a sleep so deep and so sound
that no dream version of them
dares you to stay in bed
long after the sun calls you up.

You work them away
so late into the night
that your fingers stop itching from not touching their skin
and instead find your salvation
in the scratch of this pen on paper.

You run them away
step by step and mile by mile
until you're breathing deeply enough
that the space you made for them in your body
fills up with golden hour air instead.

You cry them away.

You laugh them away.

You love them away.

Routine

Routine is my prayer
in a religion
built on
loving myself.

Beautiful Wonderful

Today some old man on the bus
told me I was beautiful.

It had been almost a month to the day
since you broke up with me for the last time
and I needed someone new to complain to

about the broken heart on my sleeve.
So I said "thank you" instead of "go away."
He responded with absolute silence.

I thought that maybe
I should thank him again
so that he would see
I wanted to talk about it.

We could even sit down
side by side
and thumb our way through

this book of wayward poetry.
Something that has
accidentally stumbled into

a written account of what happens
when the work of fixing one heartache
forces you to mend the rest.

But instead,
"You're beautiful too"
slipped out of my mouth

and the best part
wasn't the look of
shock on his face

but the realization that I
can still call someone else
besides you
beautiful
and mean it.

Now that's a concept
for this mending heart
to rally around.

Diet Plan

I need to be with someone
who is hungry for more of me
instead of working me into her diet plan.

Away Part II

Last night
my sheep and I talked so late into the night
that we saw the first glimpse of morning.

The sun
of course
had a few things to say.

It turns out
that distraction never works well
when healing broken pieces of yourself.

Especially when that distraction is used
under the guise of
self improvement.

They told me the only work
that truly heals you
is the honest kind.

The down in the dirt
and long hours in the kitchen kind.

The gentle
forgiving
nurtured by daylight
and cradled by moonlight kind.

It also turns out
that not really knowing where to start
can be the best starting place of all.

Find your broken pieces.
Invite them all inside.
Set them out.
One by one.
Hold each part up to the light.

Feel the weight of their presence in every room.

Let them become
Your new first, last and middle names.

When those broken pieces ask you
To wear your ex's t-shirt to bed
Do it

Wear it for as long as they need you to
On their command,
cut your toxic relatives out of every photo you can find.

Set fire to the church that conned you into believing
that you should hate the gay out of your body.
Forgive the part of yourself that tried.

Cry when they need you to
or when they want you to
and especially when it seems like you shouldn't.
Bargain with them.
Rage against them.
Mourn their rough edges.

Remind them that
even in their breaking
and maybe even because of it

you love them.
you love them.
you love them.

Rest Stop

I hope you keep that card
I wrote you for your birthday
where I listed 27 things that make you wonderful

and where I signed off by writing
that I was excited to meet
the next 27 after that.

It was a promise to you
that I could stay
and a pledge to myself
that I could want to.

I hope you keep that card
because the day I wrote it
I sat on a commuter train for hours
nestled in the middle seat
between Frozen and Procrastinating
because I was

Petrified
to allow myself the love required
to write 5 things, let alone dozens.

But when I started
gently hanging pieces of my happiness
on the loops and curves and edges of your name

I wrote more than 100.
I hope you keep that card
not because I want you to fill up on

any validation or compliments from me,
but because I want you to use it
as a rest stop

and as a rallying cry
on your journey to the place
where you unendingly write your own;

a place where you don't need to ask me
for numbers 28 through 100
because you already know each one.

But it if helps you to remember
that someone else can write 100 about you too
I'll gladly hold onto them.

Sarah Hulsman is a writer and producer based in Los Angeles. Born and raised in the Bay Area, she earned her B.A. in Media Studies at University of San Francisco and her M.F.A. in Film and Television Producing at Chapman University. She enjoys running to Broadway soundtracks, prefers dogs over cats, and should definitely spend more of her time reading the LGBTQ+ fiction novels piling up on her nightstand.

Sarah started writing the beginnings of Tiny Anchors immediately after drafting and deleting multiple texts to an ex girlfriend. With each poem, she felt better instead of worse, so she kept at it.

Every line in this chapbook, whether it sobs or screams or questions or envies or laughs, ultimately serves as validation: it's okay to feel "too much"; it's okay to figure out you're gay "too late"; it's okay to give your feelings the space and attention they deserve.

Great things will happen when you do.

www.ingramcontent.com/pod-product-compliance
Lightning Source LLC
LaVergne TN
LVHW041504070426
835507LV00012B/1320